FINANCIAL AFFIRMATIONS JOURNAL

Positive Affirmations for Financial Prosperity and Abundance

Angelia Brown

Table of Contents

First Things First 2
Giving Unlocks the Windows of Heaven......... 6
Get Focus and Committed 8
The Journey Begins 12
Daily Affirmations 14
Daily Journal 26

First Things First

"What you speak about, you bring about. If you don't want to see it, then don't say it." This has been my motto for many years. Once I began to press the reset button and reprogram my mind to believe for financial success and prosperity, I begin to see my finances improve. It can happen for you too.

Words are like seeds. When you speak them, they get rooted into your heart and whatever you have in your heart, becomes your life. Like I said, "What you speak about you bring about". Say it with me, "What you speak about you bring about." Your goal over the next 90 days is to develop a habit of speaking positive words and releasing your faith to cause those words to get rooted in your heart.

I encourage you to be very careful about what you are watching on TV as well as what you are listening to. I am extremely careful about the types of music I listen to as well as the shows that I watch on TV. It's important that you are very strict about this because when you expose yourself to negativity and doubt, it takes root in your heart and mind. Always remember, what gets rooted in your subconscious mind becomes a reality in your life. I am not saying go in a closet and separate yourself from the world. I am saying be mindful of what you are exposing yourself to. Negativity affects your harvest and is counterproductive. It can and does affect the results in your life. What you put before your eyes, allow your ears to hear and what you speak, becomes your life. Always remember that.

When I was in my teens and early 20s, I wasn't conscious about the words that I was speaking. To be honest, I was very negative in what I spoke as well as how I thought. I was very pessimistic about a lot of things even though, I worked hard and wanted the best for my life. I didn't realize how my words and thinking were negatively impacting the results I was getting. I felt like I was spinning on a hamster wheel getting nowhere fast. It seemed like no matter how hard I tried. I was not making progress. It was like I was trapped in a web and couldn't get out. I used to say, "When it rains it pours….. Bad things always happen to good people….. Only lucky people win…. Good things never happen for me….. I never get any breaks… Good things come to those who wait… I could go on and on. I am sure some of those sayings are familiar to you as well. You probably say them now.

    I had a wakeup call regarding the power of my words. One day, I came across a few scriptures that got my attention. You know how you have something that really speaks to you. It stops you in your tracks. Well this particular day it was like the words were jumping off the pages. I felt like God was really trying to get my attention. I was very familiar with the scriptures and could quote them at the drop of a hat. I had them memorized, but they were not alive in my heart. Proverbs 18:21 KJV, *"Death and life are in the power of the tongue; and they that love it shall eat the fruit thereof"*. What??? You mean to tell me my words can produce life and they can produce death. Talk about eye-opening. YOU have the POWER to produce LIFE. Did you hear me? When situations seem unfavorable, you can speak positive words to give life to dead and hopeless situations. Your faith-filled words are full of power to change your life for the better.

    The next scripture was Luke 6:45 NLT, *"A good person produces good things from the treasury of a good heart, and an evil person produces evil things from the treasury of an evil heart. What you say flows from what is in your heart"*. A question came to my mind after reading that verse. "If you change what gets into your heart, would that produce a better outcome for your life?" I studied deeper and came across more scriptures to confirm that you can change what the heart produces.

Proverbs 4:23 KJV, *"Keep they heart with all diligence; for out of it are the issues of life".*

Proverbs 23:7a KJV, *"For as a man thinketh in his heart, so is he".*

If you can change what is in your heart, you can change your future. When your heart is filled with abundance that means you are speaking, hearing and visioning it; you will change your financial outcome. If you want to change your current financial situation, you have to change your mindset. Change isn't change until you change. Yes. You are responsible for your change. You hold the key to your financial breakthrough. The key is pressing the reset button. Some people are sitting around waiting on God to do it. He is waiting on you. He has given you all the resources of the earth to be prosperous and excel. You have been blessed with all spiritual blessings in heavenly places. Now you must implement new success habits and disciplines to help drive your life to financial freedom.

Lasting change does not happen overnight. So that is why I have this journal to help you speak affirmations daily and begin to write positive thoughts, ideas and strategies to help you position yourself for financial increase. You will begin each day with a positive affirmation. Also notice that there is blank space on each page for you to write in the journal. It is important for you to write in the journal each day.

Giving Unlocks the Windows of Heaven

In the beginning, God set the universe in order. He instituted certain laws for the universe to operate within. For example, what goes up must come down because of the law of gravity. If you jump off a building without a parachute, you will fall at a rate of speed of 9.80665 m/s2. It doesn't matter how hard you believe you are able to defy gravity, if you jump off a building, chances are you will hit the ground. You just might meet your maker.

Another law of the universe that we are familiar with, is the law of seed time and harvest. If you sow into the right soil, cultivate the ground, you will soon see the seeds bud and you are able to reap the harvest. Now the laws regarding giving are no different than the other laws of the universe. How you employ these laws will determine the results you get in your life. Good or Bad. There is no way around it. You can't fake out the universe and expect to get something different than what you put out. The good news is, if you make the proper adjustments, you will begin to cause things to turnaround in your finances.

The foundation of your financial breakthrough is built on sowing and reaping. I equate sowing to giving. The bible says in Luke 6:38 (NKJV),

> ***Give, and it will be given to you: good measure, pressed down, shaken together, and running over will be put into your bosom. For with the same measure that you use, it will be measured back to you."***

If a farmer wants income, he doesn't just pray about it and wish for money to come. He takes that bag of seed, plant the seed, cultivate the ground and that will bring forth a harvest. If you want change in your finances, your goal is to ensure that you are planting financial seed to reap a financial harvest.

I am not saying go around and just give all your money away. You definitely have to use wisdom because some people really try to take advantage of you. I am saying, find opportunities to be a blessing to others. You can trace your harvest from what you are giving. So if you want to be intentional about reaping a financial harvest, I encourage you to give without grudging. That means you have a good attitude about giving. There are so many ways to bless people. You can give to your local church, local charities, buy food for your local food pantries, buy school supplies and clothing for needy children, help someone pay their rent, feed the homeless, etc. There are so many opportunities to sow financial seed to help others. We are blessed to be a blessing. So activate the law of increase by giving.

Prayer to develop a heart of giving:

> *Heavenly Father, I ask that you will help me become a cheerful giver. I want to be a blessing to others as you are blessing me. I remove all feeling of selfishness and greed from my life. I release all negative feelings that I have regarding giving and even those that have taken advantage of me in the past. I open my heart to giving as your word has instructed me. Direct my path to the right people to be a blessing to. I thank you for all that you are doing in my life now. I am blessed to be a blessing.*

Get Focused and Committed

Focus is imperative to your success. When I see the word focus, I have trained my mind to see, Forever On Course Until Successful. It means that you have a target to reach and you will not allow any distractions to take you off course. You don't give up, cave in or quit until you reach your goals. Why is focus key in our success? Let's start with the definition from Merriam-Webster dictionary;

> **Focus:** Adjustment for distinct vision; *also* The area that may be seen distinctly or resolved into a clear image. A point of concentration.

As you are developing new habits, you typically get distracted easier or get off course. You have the desire to live better, but your motivation is challenged during the process. As you continue to adapt your way of thinking and your lifestyle to mirror the new habit, it just seems to get easier and easier to execute. Have you ever written down new year's resolutions or verbally made them? Of course you have. One of the most popular resolutions is, "I am going to lose weight". So you start,

- **Day 1:** Things are going well. You eat healthy and exercise.
- **Day 2:** You brought your healthy lunch and will exercise after work. You feel good but you are tempted to cheat on your diet because your coworker brings donuts for everyone to enjoy. You say well it's not going to hurt to eat this one donut.
- **Day 3**: Your family wants to dine at your favorite restaurant. You decide that you will join them and get your exercise in the next day.
- *Let's fast forward......* **Day 10** You don't feel like exercising and you are making every excuse for not eating healthy. You have put off your goal until the

next year and maybe in the future you will get the weight off.

Been there, did that and have the T'shirt. Does this sound familiar? Well you might be someone that can set off on the journey and accomplish your goals without distractions. Unfortunately, many people struggle with consistency and therefore they end up quitting. We desire change but fail in the execution. Consistency is the key to the break through. The more you stick to the plan and focus on your goals, you will accomplish them. I encourage you to say your affirmations and write in your journal every day for the next 100 days. What you are doing is developing good habits that will put you in position to WIN and I mean WIN big.

I am a firm believer in writing down your goals or setting a daily reminder on your calendar or smart phone. This helps keep the goals before your eyes. That way you can't forget about them. I also like to write out a commitment and sign it. That way I hold myself accountable to doing my part in reaching my goals and I know what I am committing to. As you begin your journey of success and prosperity, you want to make a commitment to a daily success regimen. That way you have a daily plan of action.

On the next page, I have a contract that I want you to read and sign. I will also leave a few lines for you to add to the contract. Everyone is different and in different places of their journey so I don't want to dictate to you what your plan looks like. But I want to help guide you in the right direction. So I want you to read and sign the contract. Feel free to put the contract in a place that you can see it every day. Make copies and place it on your bathroom mirror, refrigerator, desk at work, etc. This will be a daily reminder that you are committed to the basic actions to create success and financial prosperity.

Commitment to Living a Successful Life

I _____ make a commitment to living a successful and productive life. I will work daily on my success regimen and do my part. I will live a life of no excuses. I will do what is necessary to live my dreams. I am willing to make the necessary sacrifices to reap the reward. I will

* Speak positive affirmations daily.
* Write in my success journal daily.
* Read a book at least 20 minutes a day.
* Not participate in gossip or backbiting.
* Always give my BEST effort when executing task.
* Remain positive all the time.
* Provide solutions versus complaints.
* Invest in my personal and professional development.
* Treat others with respect.
* Make wise financial choices.
* Contribute tithes and offerings to my local church.
* Give to the needy.
* Operate in integrity.
* Be honest in business and on my job.
* Set goals and accomplish them in a timely manner.
* Recognize distractions and not get off course.
* Make time to do things that I enjoy.
* Spend time with my family and those that I care about.
* Keep my priorities in order.

* _____
* _____
* _____

Signed: _____

The Journey Begins NOW

To change your situation, there are 3 key areas that you must focus on. These areas must be adjusted and calibrated for success
- Your mindset
- Your vision
- Your speaking

Nothing just happens. As you spend time implementing a new success regimen on a daily basis, you will see a shift in your thinking. This shift in thinking will result in a shift in your actions. The shift in your actions will change your financial outcome. This will give birth to financial increase.

When you begin to sow seeds for prosperity and abundance, you will reap the harvest from what you sow. My mother used to say, "What you sow you reap." Of course it was after we were disobedient. It was like her scare tactic. Well it worked. I would imagine a good angel on my right shoulder and the bad angel on my left shoulder. It was imprinted in my mind if you want to see good, then you want to do good. I now relate that saying to every area of my life. If you sow good, you reap good. If you sow for financial prosperity, you reap financial prosperity. If you sow good seed, you will reap a good harvest. Remember, NO SEED equals NO HARVEST. I put that in all caps because many times people feel they are entitled to success and prosperity. Just because you have been on your job or held a position for a certain number of years, does not entitle you to a promotion or raise. Many people don't want to put the work in necessary to reap the reward. The universe doesn't work that way. You must pay the price in full to reap the reward. It's a law of the universe.

Let me give you an example to clarify my point. If you have a farmer, that doesn't plant seed. He just speaks, "I believe I am going to get an abundant harvest". He says that every day and doesn't spend time planting, he should NOT expect a harvest. Neither should you. The intensity of your actions gives birth to miracles and manifestations. You can't say you believe without showing your belief. Let me say that again, you can't say you believe without also showing that you believe. Your actions are an expression of your belief.

Speaking helps to transform your mind. As your mindset is transformed, you must apply action to get lasting results. So we speak in faith and apply corresponding action that aligns with what we are affirming. We don't want to be a one hit wonder when it comes to financial prosperity. You want to be an overwhelming success.

You purchasing this book and saying affirmations demonstrates to the universe that you are ready for change. God is your source and your supply. He has the universe in the palm of his hands. When you go in the direction of change, God will assist you with making it happen.

It is my prayer that during the next 90 Days, you will see the importance of speaking positive words. I want you to write in your journal daily, train your mind to think good thoughts and implement the ideas / strategies that will be revealed to you. I would love to hear about your progress and how this journal has impacted your life. Please feel free to contact me with your testimonials at coachangelia@gmail.com.

Your Success Partner,
Angelia Brown

Daily Affirmations for Financial Prosperity and Abundance

Repeat Affirmations Aloud 2-3 times a day

"I am EXPERIENCING all the WONDERFUL things that God has in store for me."

"My FUTURE is not determined by my past. I press forward to reach my FULL POTENTIAL."

"My STEPS are ORDERED by the Lord. My heart, mind and emotions are receptive and obedient to His DIVINE instruction."

"TODAY I am doing things that GLORIFY God. I am FRUITFUL in all that I do."

"New DOORS of opportunity are always OPENING for me."

"I am always at the RIGHT place at the RIGHT time to experience the BEST that life has to offer me."

"I experience BREAKTHROUGH in my life TODAY."

"I make a conscious EFFORT to SPEAK good things out of my mouth, therefore I see GOOD things take place in my life."

"My hands are BLESSED and everything I do PROSPERS."

"I am well able to ACCOMPLISH all that I DESIRE."

"I am DEBT FREE."

"My INCOME is NOT limited. I am always PROSPERING financially."

"All BARRIERS and obstacles that affect my financial PROSPERITY are removed NOW."

"I have a PROSPERITY and ABUNDANCE mindset."

"I give THANKS for a SUBSTANTIAL INCREASE in my financial income NOW."

"LARGE sums of MONEY and financial GIFTS come to me NOW."

"I REMOVE all negative thoughts and LIMITING beliefs regarding my financial PROSPERITY."

"God's WEALTH is FLOWING in my life like a TIDAL wave."

"All of my NEEDS and DESIRES are meet instantaneously."

"I INVITE the wealth of the universe to MANIFEST abundant RICHES into my life NOW."

"My Income INCREASES every YEAR without fail."

"My words are POWERFUL and I ACTIVATE the law of ABUNDANCE and INCREASE to work for me."

"I WILL continue to remain POSITIVE when faced with ADVERSITY."

"I will NOT allow bad situations to BRING out the WORST in me."

"I know this SITUATION will not last and I will BE BETTER in the end."

"I live a STRONG, VICTORIOUS, God-centered life."

"I LIVE my life in ALIGNMENT with God's word."

"I allow God's WISDOM to LEAD and DIRECT me."

"I have great PEACE because I know that GOD WILL NEVER leave me nor forsake me."

"I PURPOSE to LIVE a life pleasing to God."

"I am a person that others can DEPEND on. I always HONOR my word."

"I OPERATE in INTEGRITY with everyone that I deal with today."

"I am a BLESSING to those CONNECTED to me."

"I always make STRIDES to IMPROVE myself."

"I SPEND time daily READING and LISTENING to things that help me GROW."

"I have UNSHAKEABLE faith in the PERFECT outcome."

"Through hard trials and tests I am DETERMINED to STAND in FAITH and not waver."

"I READ my bible, meditate on God's word, and SPEND time in prayer and worship on a daily basis."

"I know that procrastination means stagnation. Therefore, I TAKE ACTION today to reach my GOALS."

"I am always STRIVING and MOVING forward."

"My life is PROGRESSING in the RIGHT direction."

"I have the INCREASE and FAVOR of God FLOODING all my business endeavors."

"I let go of all my past disappointments and setbacks. I RELEASE all that have offended me. Today, I CHOOSE to walk in FORGIVENESS."

"I was created to ACCOMPLISH great things and make an IMPACT in the LIVES of others around me."

"Today, I make a COMMITMENT to LIVE out my full POTENTIAL."

"I have the POWER to CHANGE my current SITUATION and I no longer accept struggle as a way of LIVING for me."

"I EXPERIENCE a sudden TURNAROUND in my LIFE over the next 90 Days."

"I am BOLD and COURAGEOUS. I will no longer allow fear or doubt to prevent me from LIVING my dreams."

"I REFUSE to accept FAILURE as an option for me. I know that I WIN."

"I am NOT discouraged by challenges or obstacles that come my way. Therefore, I BELIEVE for the PERFECT outcome."

"I am willing to WORK HARD, PAY THE PRICE IN FULL, and make the necessary SACRIFICES to REAP success."

"I MAKE healthy lifestyle CHOICES. I get rid of negative HABITS that bring me down."

"I always MAKE the changes necessary to have ABUNDANT health, youth and vitality. I live a long SATISFYING healthy life."

"My MOUTH is a WELL of life. The words that I SPEAK are full of ENERGIZING power and make a lasting POSITIVE impact."

"I will NEVER be BROKE again another day in my life."

"I always have MORE than enough MONEY to meet all of my financial obligations."

"I am EXTRAORDINARY. I have the EDGE and the It FACTOR. I NEVER settle with being average."

"I NEVER get discouraged and quit because of what someone said. I use that as MOTIVATION to push harder and ACCOMPLISH my goals."

"I smile with CONFIDENCE because I know that there is a SUDDEN turnaround taking place for me NOW."

"I make a COMMITMENT to make WISE financial CHOICES. I never spend money on things that cause a financial burden to me or my family."

"I REFUSE to give up, cave in, or quit until I REACH my goals."

"I know exactly what I want in my life and FOCUS my ENERGIES on ACHIEVING realistic goals."

"I ATTRACT loving, nurturing and supportive PEOPLE into my life."

"I REMOVE all negative and TOXIC people out of my life."

"When I FACE challenges or obstacles in my life, I will not get discouraged and quit. I use my obstacles as STEPPING stones to PROPEL my life to the NEXT LEVEL."

"I always have the RIGHT attitude. I am always in CONTROL of my attitude and emotion."

"The FAVOR of God is on my life creating OPPORTUNITIES to make my life GREAT."

"Favor is OPENING doors for me TODAY."

"Today, I am BLESSED in all my endeavors. Things are REVERSED and REARRANGED to work in my favor because of the blessing on my life."

"I am a MAGNET that ATTRACTS the BEST that life has to offer me."

"I will CONTINUE to remain POSITIVE when faced with adversity."

"I live in the overflow."

I have the FAVOR, resources, wisdom, knowledge, understanding, divine strategy, divine connection, money making ideas and influence to earn 3 times the amount of money I earned last year.

"I will NOT allow a bad situation to bring out the worst in me. I know this SITUATION will not last and I will be BETTER in the end."

"I have UNSHAKEABLE faith. Through hard trials and test, I am DETERMINED to stand in faith and not bow to defeat."

"I am a FAITHFUL tither and giver. I always look for opportunities to GIVE to others."

"I am always POSITIVE and have a GREAT attitude."

"I am always at PEACE and I am a PEACE MAKER."

"I am a MULTI-MILLIONAIRE. I implement money making ideas that produce multi-million dollar results."

"I am HIGHLY FAVORED therefore people go out of their way to be a BLESSING to me."

"I am well ESTABLISHED. I am NOT wavering."

"I am WITTY and full of IDEAS and divine STRATEGY."

"I am VICTORIOUS in all things."

"I am an OFFICER of EXCELLENCE."

"I am ACTION oriented. I know that FAITH without works will never produce the results I desire."

"I MENTOR others and help them MOVE their life FORWARD."

"I am FULL of the GOLD dust of HEAVEN."

"I ACCOMPLISH task with EASE."

"I am a RICH child of my loving heavenly father. I accept all of his GOODNESS into my life NOW."

"I am MANIFESTING the life that I desire."

"I make DIVINE connections that PROPEL my life FORWARD."

"I experience divine RESTORATION in my life."

"All of my RELATIONSHIPS are BLESSED."

"I receive a PROMOTION and Financial increase over the next 90 Days."

"I OWN residential and commercial real estate PROPERTY."

"I OWN houses and land."

"I get the BEST DEALS on all my purchases."

"I am created by God to PROSPER and MAKE a positive IMPACT in this world."

"I know that setbacks are an OPPORTUNITY for a huge comeback."

"I am a LEADER and I am always ADVANCING in my career."

"I provide tremendous VALUE in the MARKETPLACE."

"I ENJOY what I do for a living. I enjoy life to the FULLEST."

"God is doing EXCEEDINGLY, ABUNDANTLY beyond all that I could ever THINK."

Debt Cancelation Accelerator

"I tell you the truth, you can say to this mountain, 'May you be lifted up and thrown into the sea,' and it will happen. But you must really believe it will happen and have no doubt in your heart." Mark 11:23 (New Living Translation)

If you have faith as small as a mustard seed, you can speak to a mountain and it will obey you. I know sometimes people think those are just bible stories. I am a firm believer in the word of God and apply the word to every area of my life. Some people may call me deep but I will tell you this, God puts HIS word above his name. That means that you can stand on the word of God and believe in his promises and it will come to pass in your life.

While I was working my 6-figure corporate job, it was easy for me to trust the Lord because I had everything working for me. After, I was evicted from my townhouse, cars repossessed and was practically homeless for 1.5 years, I had to put the word of God to the test. I lost everything and desperately desired things to turn around for my daughter and I. I felt like my life was cursed. This church girl had to get the bible out and find scriptures that I could stand on and release my faith for the turnaround. I applied Mark 11:23 to my debt and begin to see favor and debt cancelation take place in my life.

You must make a list of all your debtors and the amount you owe. You will say this affirmation over your debts while releasing your faith for supernatural debt cancelation. I encourage you to say the affirmation daily until you are 100% debt free. Now don't go out and get more debt. It's important to use the wisdom of God and as the bible says to owe no man nothing but to love him. I hope you catch that.

Debtor Name	Amount Owed
_____	$_____
_____	$_____
_____	$_____
_____	$_____
_____	$_____
_____	$_____
_____	$_____
_____	$_____
_____	$_____
_____	$_____

Debt Cancelation Accelerator Affirmation

Repeat aloud and say it with conviction in your heart: Heavenly Father, you are the great deliverer and you said that if I call upon you, that you would deliver me. I ask that you will deliver me out of my debt. I ask that you cause unexpected income to come and financial miracles to come. I ask that I have debt removing favor on my life from this day forward.

(Use the list from the previous page and say the affirmation below. Say this affirmation daily until you are out of debt.)

I speak to this mountain of debt and I command it to be removed and cast into the sea. I experience divine favor with my debtor _____ and my debtor of $_____ is release and canceled now. The spirit of debt and lack no longer control my life and I am no longer a slave to my lender. I experience supernatural debt cancelation and favor. I command this balance to decrease to zero now. I am out of debt, my needs are met and I have plenty of money in my checking, savings, retirement, and investment accounts. I no longer use debt as a way to live above my means. I am debt free NOW. I release my faith to make debt freedom a reality for me.

Speak Life Over Your Future

Repeat aloud and say it with conviction in your heart: Proverbs 13:2 says, that a man shall eat by the fruit of his mouth. Today, I make a conscious effort to speak good things out of my mouth, therefore I will eat good things, have good things and I am satisfied. I am the head and not the tail. I am always on the top and never at the bottom. I excel and advance quickly in all my endeavors. I am blessed on my way in and blessed on my way out. I am blessed where ever I go and in whatever I am involved in. I will never be broke again another day in my life because I live in the overflow. My heavenly Father is always supplying my needs according to his riches in glory. Therefore, I lack no good thing, because I trust solely in him. Blessings are upon my head because I trust the Lord with all my heart. Everything that I put my hands to prospers and excels because the favor of God floods my life. My labor always produces a profit for me. I am diligent and always operate in excellence in my business affairs. I am wealthy and prosperous in every area of my life. I believe I receive it and I release my faith to bring this to pass in my life NOW.

Daily Journal

Why is journaling important? Journaling allows you the ability to articulate your thoughts and success strategies on paper. You must get in the habit of getting your thoughts out of your head and put them into an action plan. This allows you the ability to take the idea from just being thoughts to becoming your reality.

What should you write about in your daily journal?
- How is the affirmation impacting your view of your financial future?
- How the affirmation has affected how you think?
- What changes you need to make to improve your financial situation?
- Business ideas that come to mind.
- Levels of income you want to accomplish.
- Write your goals, dreams and aspirations.
- Results you are seeing in your life.
- Places you want to travel to when you achieve financial freedom
- New people that you are meeting that will help you on your success journey.
- Motivation Quotes, Scriptures, etc.
- Fears you are overcoming.
- Personal Development Goals: Books, Conferences, Training, etc
- Add pictures of dreams and goals. Example: Dream Car, Dream House, Vacation Destinations, franchises, career levels, ranks achieved in your company, etc

What **NOT** to write about in your journal:
- Thoughts of failure
- Negative situations that happened during the day
- Reflecting on your past and why you are not further along.
- NO NEGATIVITY
- ABSOLUTELY NO Complaining
- Gossip or speaking negative about others

Note: Your journal is not a trash can so don't put any trash in your journal. Remember negativity is counterproductive to your financial increase.

Repeat aloud, **"I am *EXPERIENCING* all the WONDERFUL things that God has in store for me."**

Repeat aloud, **"My *FUTURE* is not determined by my past. I press forward to reach my *FULL POTENTIAL*."**

_____

_____

_____

_____

_____

_____

_____

_____

_____

_____

_____

_____

Repeat aloud, **"My *STEPS* are ORDERED by the Lord. My heart, mind and emotions are receptive and obedient to His DIVINE instruction."**

Repeat aloud, **"TODAY I am doing things that *GLORIFY* God. I am *FRUITFUL* in all that I do."**

Repeat aloud, **"New *DOORS* of opportunity are always *OPENING* for me."**

_____

_____

_____

_____

_____

_____

_____

_____

_____

_____

_____

_____

_____

Repeat aloud, **"I am always at the *RIGHT* place at the *RIGHT* time to experience the *BEST* that life has to offer me."**

Repeat aloud, **"I experience BREAKTHROUGH in my life TODAY."**

Repeat aloud, **"I make a conscious *EFFORT* to *SPEAK* good things out of my mouth, therefore I see *GOOD* things take place in my life."**

_____
_____
_____
_____
_____
_____
_____
_____
_____
_____
_____
_____

Repeat aloud, **"My hands are *BLESSED* and everything I do *PROSPERS*."**

Repeat aloud, **"I am well able to *ACCOMPLISH* all that I *DESIRE*."**

Repeat aloud, **"I am DEBT FREE."**

Repeat aloud, **"My *INCOME* is *NOT* limited. I am always *PROSPERING* financially."**

Repeat aloud, **"All *BARRIERS* and obstacles that affect my financial *PROSPERITY* are removed NOW."**

Repeat aloud, **"I have a PROSPERITY and ABUNDANCE mindset."**

Repeat aloud, **"I give *THANKS* for a *SUBSTANTIAL INCREASE* in my financial income *NOW*."**

_____

_____

_____

_____

_____

_____

_____

_____

_____

_____

_____

_____

_____

_____

Repeat aloud, **"*LARGE* sums of *MONEY* and financial *GIFTS* come to me NOW."**

_____
_____
_____
_____
_____
_____
_____
_____
_____
_____
_____
_____
_____

Repeat aloud, **"I *REMOVE* all negative thoughts and *LIMITING* beliefs regarding my financial *PROSPERITY.*"**

_____

_____

_____

_____

_____

_____

_____

_____

_____

_____

_____

Repeat aloud, **"God's WEALTH is FLOWING in my life like a TIDAL wave."**

Repeat aloud, **"All of my NEEDS and DESIRES are meet instantaneously."**

_____
_____
_____
_____
_____
_____
_____
_____
_____
_____
_____
_____
_____
_____
_____

Repeat aloud, **"I INVITE the wealth of the universe to MANIFEST abundant RICHES into my life."**

_____

_____

_____

_____

_____

_____

_____

_____

_____

_____

_____

_____

Repeat aloud, **"My Income INCREASES every YEAR without fail."**

_____
_____
_____
_____
_____
_____
_____
_____
_____
_____
_____
_____
_____
_____
_____
_____

Repeat aloud, **"My words are POWERFUL and I ACTIVATE the law of ABUNDANCE and INCREASE to work for me."**

_____

_____

_____

_____

_____

_____

_____

_____

_____

_____

_____

_____

Repeat aloud, **"I *WILL* continue to remain *POSITIVE* when faced with *ADVERSITY*."**

_____

_____

_____

_____

_____

_____

_____

_____

_____

_____

_____

_____

_____

Repeat aloud, **"I know this *SITUATION* will not last and I will *BE BETTER* in the end."**

_____
_____
_____
_____
_____
_____
_____
_____
_____
_____
_____
_____
_____
_____

Repeat aloud, **"I live a *STRONG*, *VICTORIOUS*, God-centered life."**

Repeat aloud, **"I *LIVE* my life in *ALIGNMENT* with God's word."**

Repeat aloud, **"I allow God's *WISDOM* to *LEAD* and *DIRECT* me."**

Repeat aloud, **"I have great *PEACE* because I know that *GOD WILL NEVER* leave me nor forsake me."**

Repeat aloud, **"I am a *BLESSING* to those *CONNECTED* to me."**

_____
_____
_____
_____
_____
_____
_____
_____
_____
_____
_____
_____
_____
_____
_____

Repeat aloud, **"I have *UNSHAKEABLE* faith in the *PERFECT* outcome."**

Repeat aloud, **"Through hard trials and tests I am DETERMINED to STAND in FAITH and not waver."**

_____
_____
_____
_____
_____
_____
_____
_____
_____
_____
_____
_____
_____
_____

Repeat aloud, **"I know that procrastination means stagnation. Therefore, I *TAKE ACTION* today to reach my *GOALS*."**

_____
_____
_____
_____
_____
_____
_____
_____
_____
_____
_____
_____
_____
_____

Repeat aloud, **"I am always STRIVING and MOVING forward."**

Repeat aloud, **"My life is *PROGRESSING* in the *RIGHT* direction."**

Repeat aloud, **"I have the *INCREASE* and *FAVOR* of God *FLOODING* all my business endeavors."**

Repeat aloud, **"I let go of all my past disappointments and setbacks. I *RELEASE* all that have offended me. Today, I *CHOOSE* to walk in *FORGIVENESS.*"**

_____

_____

_____

_____

_____

_____

_____

_____

_____

_____

_____

Repeat aloud, **"I was created to ACCOMPLISH great things and make an IMPACT in the LIVES of others around me."**

Repeat aloud, **"Today, I make a COMMITMENT to *LIVE* out my full *POTENTIAL*."**

Repeat aloud, **"I have the *POWER* to *CHANGE* my current *SITUATION* and I no longer accept struggle as a way of *LIVING* for me."**

_____

_____

_____

_____

_____

_____

_____

_____

_____

_____

_____

_____

Repeat aloud, **"I *EXPERIENCE* a sudden *TURNAROUND* in my *LIFE* over the next 90 Days."**

Repeat aloud, **"I am *BOLD* and *COURAGEOUS*. I will no longer allow fear or doubt to prevent me from *LIVING* my dreams."**

_____

_____

_____

_____

_____

_____

_____

_____

_____

_____

_____

_____

_____

Repeat aloud, **"I *REFUSE* to accept *FAILURE* as an option for me. I know that I *WIN*."**

Repeat aloud, **"I am *NOT* discouraged by challenges or obstacles that come my way. Therefore, I *BELIEVE* for the *PERFECT* outcome."**

_____
_____
_____
_____
_____
_____
_____
_____
_____
_____
_____

Repeat aloud, **"I am willing to *WORK HARD*, *PAY THE PRICE IN FULL*, and make the necessary *SACRIFICES* to *REAP* success."**

_____
_____
_____
_____
_____
_____
_____
_____
_____
_____
_____
_____

Repeat aloud, **"My *MOUTH* is a *WELL* of life. The words that I *SPEAK* are full of *ENERGIZING* power and make a lasting *POSITIVE* impact."**

_____
_____
_____
_____
_____
_____
_____
_____
_____
_____
_____
_____
_____
_____

Repeat aloud, **"I will *NEVER* be *BROKE* again another day in my life."**

_____
_____
_____
_____
_____
_____
_____
_____
_____
_____
_____
_____
_____
_____
_____

Repeat aloud, **"I always have *MORE* than enough *MONEY* to meet all of my financial obligations."**

_____

_____

_____

_____

_____

_____

_____

_____

_____

_____

_____

_____

Repeat aloud, **"I *NEVER* get discouraged and quit because of what someone said. I use that as *MOTIVATION* to push harder and *ACCOMPLISH* my goals."**

_____
_____
_____
_____
_____
_____
_____
_____
_____
_____
_____
_____

Repeat aloud, **"I smile with *CONFIDENCE* because I know that there is a SUDDEN turnaround taking place for me *NOW*."**

Repeat aloud, **"I *REFUSE* to give up, cave in, or quit until I *REACH* my goals."**

Repeat aloud, **"I know exactly what I want in my life and *FOCUS* my *ENERGIES* on *ACHIEVING* realistic goals."**

_____
_____
_____
_____
_____
_____
_____
_____
_____
_____
_____
_____
_____
_____

Repeat aloud, **"When I *FACE* challenges or obstacles in my life, I will not get discouraged and quit. I use my obstacles as *STEPPING* stones to *PROPEL* my life to the *NEXT LEVEL*."**

_____
_____
_____
_____
_____
_____
_____
_____
_____
_____
_____
_____

Repeat aloud, **"I always have the *RIGHT* attitude. I am always in *CONTROL* of my attitude and emotion."**

Repeat aloud, **"The *FAVOR* of God is on my life creating *OPPORTUNITIES* to make my life *GREAT*."**

Repeat aloud, **"Favor is *OPENING* doors for me *TODAY*."**

Repeat aloud, **"Today, I am *BLESSED* in all my endeavors. Things are *REVERSED* and *REARRANGED* to work in my favor because of the blessing on my life."**

_____
_____
_____
_____
_____
_____
_____
_____
_____
_____
_____

Repeat aloud, **"I am a *MAGNET* that *ATTRACTS* the *BEST* that life has to offer me."**

_____
_____
_____
_____
_____
_____
_____
_____
_____
_____
_____
_____
_____
_____
_____

Repeat aloud, **"I will *CONTINUE* to remain *POSITIVE* when faced with adversity."**

_____

_____

_____

_____

_____

_____

_____

_____

_____

_____

_____

_____

Repeat aloud, **"I will *NOT* allow a bad situation to bring out the worst in me. I know this *SITUATION* will not last and I will be *BETTER* in the end."**

Repeat aloud, **"I live in the overflow."**

Repeat aloud, **"I have *UNSHAKEABLE* faith. Through hard trials and test, I am *DETERMINED* to stand in faith and not bow to defeat."**

_____
_____
_____
_____
_____
_____
_____
_____
_____
_____
_____
_____

Repeat aloud, **"I am a *FAITHFUL* tither and giver. I always look for opportunities to *GIVE* to others."**

_____

_____

_____

_____

_____

_____

_____

_____

_____

_____

_____

_____

Repeat aloud, **"I am always *POSITIVE* and have a *GREAT* attitude."**

_____
_____
_____
_____
_____
_____
_____
_____
_____
_____
_____
_____
_____
_____
_____
_____

Repeat aloud, **"I am always at *PEACE* and I am a *PEACE MAKER*."**

Repeat aloud, **"I am a *MULTI-MILLIONAIRE*. I implement money making ideas that produce multi-million dollar results."**

_____
_____
_____
_____
_____
_____
_____
_____
_____
_____
_____
_____

Repeat aloud, **"I am *HIGHLY FAVORED* therefore people go out of their way to be a *BLESSING* to me."**

_____
_____
_____
_____
_____
_____
_____
_____
_____
_____
_____
_____
_____
_____
_____
_____

Repeat aloud, **"I am well *ESTABLISHED*. I am *NOT* wavering."**

_____
_____
_____
_____
_____
_____
_____
_____
_____
_____
_____
_____
_____

Repeat aloud, **"I am *WITTY* and full of *IDEAS* and divine *STRATEGY*."**

_____

_____

_____

_____

_____

_____

_____

_____

_____

_____

_____

_____

_____

_____

_____

Repeat aloud, **"I am *VICTORIOUS* in all things."**

Repeat aloud, **"I am an *OFFICER* of *EXCELLENCE.*"**

Repeat aloud, **"I am *ACTION* oriented. I know that *FAITH* without works will never produce the results I desire."**

Repeat aloud, **"I *MENTOR* others and help them *MOVE* their life *FORWARD*."**

Repeat aloud, **"I am *FULL* of the *GOLD* dust of *HEAVEN*."**

Repeat aloud, **"I *ACCOMPLISH* task with *EASE.*"**

Repeat aloud, **"I am a *RICH* child of my loving heavenly father. I accept all of his *GOODNESS* into my life *NOW*."**

Repeat aloud, **"I am *MANIFESTING* the life that I desire."**

Repeat aloud, **"I make *DIVINE* connections that *PROPEL* my life *FORWARD*."**

_____
_____
_____
_____
_____
_____
_____
_____
_____
_____
_____
_____
_____
_____
_____

Repeat aloud, **"I experience divine *RESTORATION in my life.*"**

Repeat aloud, **"All of my *RELATIONSHIPS* are *BLESSED*."**

Repeat aloud, **"I receive a *PROMOTION* by the end of the year."**

Repeat aloud, **"I *OWN* residential and commercial real estate *PROPERTY*."**

Repeat aloud, **"I *OWN* houses and land."**

Repeat aloud, **"I get the *BEST DEALS* on all my purchases."**

Repeat aloud, **"I am created by God to *PROSPER* and *MAKE* a positive *IMPACT* in this world."**

Repeat aloud, **"I know that setbacks are an OPPORTUNITY for a huge comeback."**

Repeat aloud, **"I am a *LEADER* and I am always *ADVANCING* in my career and business endeavors."**

_____

_____

_____

_____

_____

_____

_____

_____

_____

_____

_____

_____

_____

Repeat aloud, **"I provide tremendous *VALUE* in the *MARKETPLACE*."**

Repeat aloud, **"I pursue my purpose passionately. I know that my life has meaning.**

_____
_____
_____
_____
_____
_____
_____
_____
_____
_____
_____
_____

Repeat aloud, **"I speak increase over my wallet, checkbook, businesses, investments."**

Repeat aloud, **"My mind is open and receptive to opportunities to grow my income substantially."**

Repeat aloud, **"I am a good steward over my finances. I make sound financial decisions."**

Prayer of Salvation

On December 20, 1993, my life would be forever changed. I accepted Jesus as Lord of my life. It was during one of the toughest times of my life and I can truly say it saved my life. I was so depressed after dealing with my mother's murder. I felt like my heart was broken into a million pieces. I had a good friend lead me through the prayer of Salvation and my life has NEVER been the same.

I want you to know that God loves you and there is a divine purpose and plan for your life. Regardless of what you have been through, your failures, shortcomings…God loves you. "For God so loved the world that he gave his only begotten son that whosoever believes in him shall not perish but have everlasting life" (John 3:16 KJV). Jesus said, "The thief does not come except to steal, and to kill and to destroy. I have come that they may have life, and that they may have it more abundantly" (John 10:10 NKJV). Your life is full and complete in God. I encourage you to totally surrender your life to him. If you would like to receive Jesus into your life as Lord and Savior, pray the following prayer out loud and mean it with true conviction in your heart:

Heavenly Father, I know I am a sinner. Today I make a conscious confession and I choose to turn from my sins. I thank you for sending your son Jesus to die on the cross for me. I confess with my mouth and believe in my heart that Jesus is the Son of God. I believe that you raised Jesus from the dead. Please, forgive me of my sins and cleans my unrighteousness. Lord Jesus I welcome you into my heart today. Be the Lord of my life. Fill me with your Holy Spirit. Teach me to walk with you and live for you all the days of my life. Thank you for saving me and for giving me the gift of eternal life in Heaven with you. Father, let your will be done in my life as it is in heaven. Amen.

If you prayed the prayer of Salvation, the angels are rejoicings and so am I. It is important to find a bible based church in your local area that you can attend regularly. This will help you grow in your relationship with God. I encourage you to pray for God to direct you to the right congregation that you can grow in your walk with the Lord. You can also purchase a bible at your local bookstore or online. Begin reading and learning all about God's precious promises that HE has for you. I wish you all the best in all your endeavors.

About the Author

Angelia Brown is an exceptional speaker, trainer and certified life coach with an unrelenting drive to help others thrive in their careers, business and personal finances. Her distinctive methods have generated  consistent results earning her a solid reputation as a results driven, natural leader. She is the owner and founder of Destiny Connectors, LLC.

With a BS in Management Information Systems and a BS in Applied Discrete Mathematics from Auburn University, Angelia's career spans across varies industries where she developed valuable skills in business analysis, project management, customer success management, social media marketing, sales and team building. Angelia's expertise has assisted countless entrepreneurs and small business owners to optimize their potential for sustainable growth, peak performance and strategic turnaround.

Angelia later decided to join a direct sales company where she was able to match her corporate 6-figure salary and quit her job to work her business full-time. It was at this stage that Angelia learned the toughest lessons in business the hard way. As a single mother, Angelia found herself evicted, cars repossessed and practically homeless, living from one hotel to another for almost two years with her young daughter. She realized that she had to employ the success principles previously learned to turn her situation around.

Her undying strength, resilience and determination equipped her to meet the challenges head on. Angelia decided to start another business and was able to restore her life. Now Angelia takes her life experiences to provide powerful lessons for success in all areas of life.

Angelia is now sought-after by individuals, churches, small business owners and corporations for speaking, workshops and training events. She is a bright, energetic, positive, visionary leader. She is favored for her no nonsense motivational coaching on how to get unstuck, strategize and develop the disciplines to create success.

Angelia continues her walk in life motivating and inspiring people to face adversity diligently and sustain laser focus on fulfilling their God given destiny.

Made in United States
Troutdale, OR
11/23/2024